SHARKS!

PHONICS

Fish Facts

Book 2: sh (Ending blend)

By Quinlan B. Lee

Photo Credits: cover: Dan Callister/Alamy; title page: Norbert Probst/Corbis; pages 2-3: Jens Kuhfs/Getty Images; page 4: Rainer von Brandis/iStockphoto; page 6: Mauricio Handler/National Geographic; page 8 solarseven/Shutterstock; pages 10-11: Charles V Angelo/Getty Images; pages 12-13: Dan Callister/Alamy; pages 14-15: switchfoot/iStockphoto; page16: DLILLC/Getty Images.

ISBN 978-0-545-74699-1

12 11 10 9 8 7 6 5 4 3 2 1   14 15 16 17 18/0

Printed in China   145

First Printing, September 2014

SCHOLASTIC INC.

Most people know sharks like to eat **fish**.

Fresh fish is their favorite **dish**.

But did you know sharks *are* **fish**?

A shark has skin like a **fish**.

A shark has fins like a **fish**.

A shark swims like a **fish**.

A shark breathes like a **fish**.

But sharks are special **fish**.

Most **fish** have hard bones.

Shark bones are soft.

They can **squish** like your nose.

Shark bones don't break

if you **smash** them.

Soft shark bones twist
and bend.
That helps the sharks **swish**
back and forth.
They can **swish** very fast.
They can catch **fish** to eat
in a **flash**!

Most **fish** have slippery scales.

Shark scales are bumpy.

If you **brush** a shark's scales,
they feel like sand.

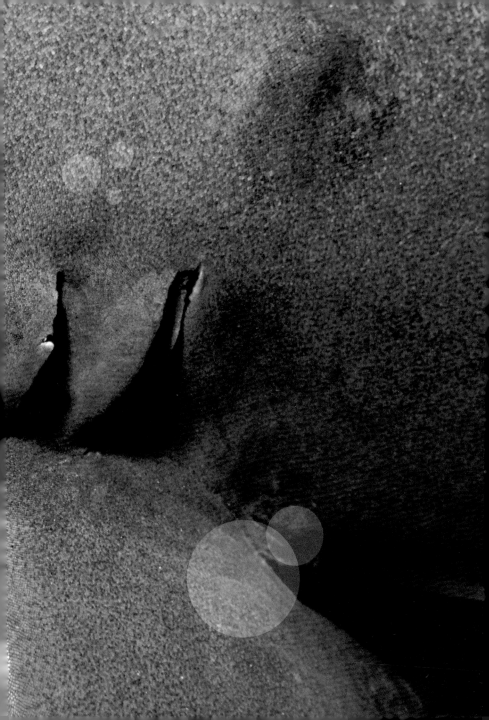

Most **fish** can jump.

Some sharks can jump very high.

Great white sharks can jump out of the water and **crash** back down with a **splash**!

Most **fish** have fins that let them swim backwards. Shark fins only let them swim forwards.

Sharks cannot **crash** into things behind them.

Some people have **fish** as pets. Would you want a shark in your **fish** tank?